THE
RHYTHM
STRING
PLAYER

STRUM BOWING IN ACTION

By Tracy Silverman

Music preparation by Tracy Silverman
Layout by Austin Gray www.entireworld.us
Painting and Drawings by Rachel Kice www.rachelkice.com

All compositions Copyright © 2022 by Tracy Silverman
All rights reserved.
ISBN 978-1-7348145-9-0

No part of this book may be reproduced or transmitted in any form or by any means, electronic or mechanical, including photocopying, recording, or by any information storage and retrieval systems without written permission from the author or publisher, except for the inclusion of brief quotations in a review.

Published by Silverman Musical Enterprises, LLC
Nashville, TN
info@tracysilverman.com | www.tracysilverman.com | www.strumbowing.com

Table of Contents

PREFACE …………………………………………………………… ii

PART 1: CHORD FUNDAMENTALS
Introduction to Rhythm String Playing …………………… 1
   1. Feelin' the Groove …………………………………… 6
   2. My Sweet Groove …………………………………… 14
   3. Dominant Strum ……………………………………… 17
   4. Honeysuckle Groove ………………………………… 18
   5. Groovin' on the Circle ……………………………… 20
   6. Groovin' Further 'Round the Circle ……………… 24
   7. Strummin' Your Way Home ………………………… 26

PART 2: STRUM BOWING IN ACTION
   8. Sly Strum ……………………………………………… 34
   9. Soul Groove …………………………………………… 41
   10. Get Up and Strum ………………………………… 43
   11. Riff Rodck …………………………………………… 46
   12. Jammin' with the Geetars ………………………… 49
   13. Cabbage Strum ……………………………………… 52
   14. Drowsy Strum ……………………………………… 55
   15. Jazz Blues in F ……………………………………… 57
   16. The Long Way Home ……………………………… 60
   17. Strum Bossa ………………………………………… 63
   18. Salsa Groove ………………………………………… 67
   19. Get Groovy …………………………………………… 70
   20. Groovy as Hell ……………………………………… 72
   21. Vibrato ……………………………………………… 74
   Closing Words ………………………………………… 80
   Glossary ………………………………………………… 82

Preface

If you are new to Strum Bowing, welcome!

This book is the sequel to *The Strum Bowing Method: How to Groove on Strings*, which means that I am going to assume that you, dear reader, will either have already read *The Strum Bowing Method* or will at any rate be comfortable with a few new terms and concepts which don't get fully explained here. Hopefully there will be enough contextual clues to make it all clear. I mean, it's not brain surgery.

One of the crucial concepts of Strum Bowing is the ghosting or muting of notes. This is an essential part of the method, because the whole idea of Strum Bowing is that you area able to play a continuous strum with your bow but not make a continuous stream of notes. Only the desired notes come out, the rest are muted or ghosted. Since this book is building on the last, I am going to assume that, even if you have not gotten comfortable with ghosting yet, you at least are aware of what it is and more or less how it's done.

It is my hope that this book will give you a handful of real-life examples of how to put the Strum Bowing concept into action in several different stylistic genres. It's just a sampler of a few of many different approaches to playing in contemporary styles, just to show what's possible and how to solve the various problems of imitating the guitar and bass in those genres.

This book is intended to be used with its accompanying etude book, *Chord Jams: Strum Bowing Etudes Book 2*. I reference the Chord Jams book in every chapter, so I am going to assume you are using both books together.

How to take Strum Bowing to the Next Level

The Rhythm String Player is where we put the concepts of Strum Bowing into real-life use.

The whole point of Strum Bowing is to give you the ability to play grooves as part of the rhythm section. But how do you actually use Strum Bowing in a tune? What does it mean to be a rhythm string player?

Now that we know how to keep time with our arm by strum bowing—something non-intuitive for classical string players—what do we actually play?

Let's break it down.

The Classical Rhythm Section

Playing rhythm on strings seems like a radical, paradigm-shifting approach to string playing. But it's not. String quartets are filled with second violin and viola parts that are the equivalent, for their time, of the rhythm section. Cellists are already very familiar with being the bass player and establishing the root of the harmony as it moves throughout a piece. It's really the first violinists who have the biggest adjustment to make from the "lead" role to the "rhythm" role, to use the guitar parlance.

There are rhythm parts written into much of classical music. Strings were often the "rhythm" instrument in the grooves of the day—grooves like gavottes and bourees and allemandes. So, playing rhythm on strings is not really new. What is new is that we will be working on rhythm parts that are not from that historical music but from our own popular music idiom.

Mozart was Hip

Unlike Mozart and Tschaikovsky, who were possibly much more hip to the fashions of their time than we might think, most string players have completely lost the connection with our own current popular musical culture. All those classical masterpieces—whether Mozart's compositions in the swinging Viennese style of the late 1700's, with its taste for Italian culture, or Tschaikovsky's Russian School that was taking Europe by storm in the late 1800's—all were written fully in the current musical style of their day.

The styles changed every generation just as the clothes changed. And strings always stayed in step with that fashion, from the 1600's thru the 1900's.

Until the 20th century.

The styles changed every generation just as the clothes changed. And strings always stayed in step with that fashion, from the 1600's thru the 1900's. Until the 20th century.

Dropping the Ball

By the early 1900's, string playing and string pedagogy had developed into a fine art with fairly narrow traditions focusing on an increasingly virtuosic repertoire. The Franco-Belgian and Russian schools had advanced the state of the art to such a high level that it reached a point of arrested development and stopped evolving naturally with the current popular styles.

For the first time, string playing became more historical than current, focusing on replaying the masterpieces of the past rather than keeping up with the current popular musical styles of the Jazz and Swing eras.

By separating itself and not evolving with the popular musical culture, string playing essentially erased itself from the popular music landscape. From the jazz age forward, strings are not really involved. The ball got dropped. Strings became irrelevant in American popular music and thereby irrelevant to 95% of school-age kids.

If someone asked you to name the typical Jazz instrument, you wouldn't say violin or cello. Same for Rock. Same for Hip Hop. Strings weren't part of any of that. (Unless we were the string section, utilized to bring an old-fashioned classical/cinematic grandeur to a track. I don't consider that an organic essential part of jazz, rock or hip hop. In fact, it proves that we are the opposite since we're brought in for the effect of contrast.)

Strings became irrelevant in American popular music and thereby irrelevant to 95% of school-age kids.

Playing Rhythm Instead of Lead

I think it's essential to close this gap and to play strings in a way that is organic to our popular musical culture. And I think the first step in that direction is to play "rhythm" rather than "lead." That's because, in order to authentically play in any style, you first need to feel the connection between the music and movement—the way it makes your body dance. Popular music is groove-based music, and, as I stated repeatedly in *The Strum Bowing Method*, "rhythmic music comes from rhythmic movement."

All we are doing here is reconnecting ourselves as string players with fully half of our musical nature—we are not just melodic instruments. We can also function as rhythm instruments just like a guitar. We can be absolutely as percussive, funky, rocking, or groove-establishing as any guitar.

And we do it in our own way, with our own accent as string players. This future of strings that I keep ranting about is a world in which string players bring what is idiomatic to strings into the sound of contemporary pop records. It's a world in which a 6-string violin can take the role of a guitar, but with a slightly different "string" vibe that finds a real place in pop music.

Strings can be absolutely as percussive, funky, rocking, or groove-establishing as any guitar.

The Future is 6-String

That's the future I'd like to see. And honestly, I believe the future will be 6-string, because of the way those 2 additional lower strings transforms the instrument into a chordal instrument like the (6-string) guitar.

There are a lot of sound reasons (pun intended) why the guitar has been one of the dominant instruments in our popular music, and one of the biggest is its range. The lower octave of the guitar is essential to establish a sense of bass notes, a necessity of any chordal instrument. So, if we want to provide the same chordal function, we need the same range.

To that end. I have included 4-, 5- and 6-string versions of each etude as well as a cello version in *Chord Jams: Strum Bowing Etudes Book 2*. Sadly, there is not a viola version. It's not that I have any issue with violas. I just think that most progressive players who are looking for this kind of instruction will probably be using 5-strings because they are already fairly ubiquitous. And it's my guess and hope that in 10-20 years, 6-strings will be just as common as 5-strings are now—and they will become fully functional chordal instruments in many bands.

It's a Guitar World, We're Just Living In It

Now, we can't reinvent the past. We missed out on the 20th century, for all intents and purposes, a few outliers like Grappelli and Ponty, etc. notwithstanding. We can't change that—inserting ourselves into those styles of the past will always be something of a curiosity: our "take" on jazz or rock; strings imitating more legitimate jazz and rock instruments like saxophones and electric guitars. We will always be outsiders in those genres—and we're never going to be legitimately recognized in them simply because we were never a part of them to begin with.

We can't rewrite history. But we can lay the groundwork to create a new future for string players.

We can demonstrate to contemporary music makers—the creators who are putting out music that is connecting with listeners all over the world—what strings can do.

It's All About the Groove

The heart of any style is its groove. There's no Jazz without the swing. There's no Hip Hop without the beats.

The instrument we are closest to in the popular musical world is the guitar, so that is going to be our model. Guitar players create the groove in their strumming arm, with a pick or with their fingers. For string players, we groove with a bow.

That's why I wrote *The Strum Bowing Method: How to Groove on Strings*. First you need a clear path to a whole new rhythmic vocabulary, updated from the string quartets of 18th and 19th century Europe to the contemporary top 40 landscape. First you need the techniques of ghosting and grooving.

And if we want anyone to take us seriously in popular musical culture, we are going to have to demonstrate some serious ability to overthrow the "strings can't swing" reputation that precedes us.

But then, how do we play chords on string instruments? How do we play like a rhythm guitar player? What does that even sound like? That's why I wrote *The Rhythm String Player: Strum Bowing in Action*.

The future for strings evolves with the future of pop music. In order to paint ourselves back into the current musical landscape, we have to be in the studios and on the records.

And if we want anyone to take us seriously in popular musical culture, especially as a rhythm player and groove maker, we are going to have to demonstrate some serious ability to overthrow the "strings can't swing" reputation that precedes us. We need to have string players who can groove on a G chord as easily as play a G scale, who can accompany someone on a blues as easily as play a Bouree.

A New Approach for Strings

This calls for a different approach to string teaching. We don't have to stop doing what we're doing in the classical world, just add to it. Add the ability to play chords. Pretty much as simple as that. The rest is 2nd and 3rd level building on that. But in its essence, playing rhythm is playing chords.

And since even being aware of chords is, unfortunately, new to many string players, especially upper string players, the first section of this book addresses a few of the more common chord formulas that you will likely encounter, from simpler to slightly more complex.

In order for strings to be a vital part of the mainstream musical future, we have to weave ourselves into the past. We need to authentically speak the language of jazz and rock and hip hop. We need to participate in the musical conversation not as someone who barely understands it, but as someone who has been speaking it all their lives, or at least fluently.

We need some skills. And we're going to get them from the guitar players.

Free Your Inner Guitar Player

Strum Bowing is all about using a bow like you're strumming a guitar. So, let's start with the given that we are modeling ourselves on our closest sibling in the pop musical landscape, the guitar. There is no shame in that.

The reason there is no shame is that we will never actually sound exactly like a rhythm guitar. It's an aspirational goal. That may seem like a curse to you as I repeatedly ask you to imitate guitars throughout this book, but it's also a blessing. It's what makes us a viable alternative to guitars—because we can do what they do but sound a little different.

I always tell students, go ahead and try to imitate your favorite artist on your violin or cello. If it's Miles, try to get his tone, his timing, his sense. Imitate your favorite licks over and over like an impersonator practicing an accent or catchphrase, til you have it down cold.

Don't worry. No one will ever mistake you for Miles.

We need to participate in the musical conversation not as someone who barely understands it, but as someone who has been speaking it all their lives, or at least fluently.

Weaving into the Musical Conversation

So, we start out by weaving our way into the musical conversation. We will learn from guitar players how to do all the things we need to do in order to be invited into the band or into the studio. String teachers, we can learn a lot from the way beginning guitar is taught: you go from this chord to that chord and keep time with your hand.

This guitar approach assumes most of the music is being improvised within a given chord progression in the form of a strum. Add your own rhythm to taste. Reading music is not necessary. Reading a chord chart is, eventually.

If you're a classical string player, you may have spent 8 hours a day perfecting Paganini caprices, but in all likelihood, how to play chords and reading chord charts were never taught to you. So, let's create a future that's different from the past. Let's dig in!

Section 1:
Chord Fundamentals

Introduction to Rhythm String Playing

Before we jump into jamming on tunes, we need to get familiar with working with chords.

Strings are taught and played primarily as melodic instruments, so we don't think about chords much. Cello and bass players are often familiar with bass notes and roots of chords, but upper string players are like sailors on a flat ocean of melody who are unaware of the chords and harmony swimming around beneath them.

Section 1: Chord Fundamentals serves two purposes:
- to teach some basic harmony to those who may not be familiar with it
- to learn it on our string instruments, not on a piano or guitar

It's important to make that connection between chords and our instruments at the earliest point possible in the learning process, simply because it's something you may never have done on your instrument before. We need to develop new muscle memory.

We will look at the idea of resolving by fifths, (the V-I resolution,) which is the driving force behind all western harmony—dominant chords, secondary dominants (ii-V-I) and the Circle of Fifths. This is the background you will need for Section 2, because we will soon be using these chord progressions as we dig into specific genres and how to be a rhythm player in those different styles.

Upper string players are like sailors on a flat ocean of melody who are unaware of the chords and harmony swimming around beneath them.

Key Concepts of Rhythm String Playing

So, as an intro to rhythm string playing, here are a few of the key concepts of playing rhythm on strings.

Playing Chords

The goal is to be able to accompany other musicians by playing rhythm. When we talk about backing someone up and playing chords, that means playing the bass notes as well as other chord tones and doing it in a rhythm that's appropriate to the style. It means reading a chord chart and making up a part.

Playing chords is a paradigm shift in how strings are played, because strings are taught and played generally as melodic instruments. We don't learn how to play chords like guitar players do. We are not considered a chordal instrument because our instruments aren't designed to play many strings at the same time.

But...

We can easily arpeggiate and essentially "fingerpick" chordal patterns using the rhythmic motor of Strum Bowing. We learned about chopping and what I refer to as a 3-D Strum in The Strum Bowing Method. Now that we have developed the ability to do a 3-D Strum, to play a chord in rhythm, how do we apply it?

For a musician, harmony is all about how these harmonious or dissonant overtones makes us feel. It's not dry theory—it's physical, baby!

Many string players have very little understanding of harmony and how chords work. So, first let's break it down:

The Physics of Harmony

First of all, it often seems like a lot of theory and rules when you are new to it, but I find it helpful, especially as a string player, to remember that it's not arbitrary—there are simple physics in the harmonic series of overtones that cause things to sound the way they do, which we can categorize as Consonance and Dissonance. We just organize that into usable patterns, such as chords and scales. It is not at all a dry and academic subject—for a musician, harmony is all about how these harmonious or dissonant overtones makes us feel. Songwriters and composers have always used the psychoacoustics of chord progressions to play with our emotions. It's not dry theory—it's physical, baby!

Consonance and Dissonance

- Consonance is when the harmonic series is stable. The overtones are aligned and resonate harmoniously, (frequencies tend to reinforce other frequencies.)
- Dissonance is when the harmonic series is unstable. There are overtones that are in conflict with other overtones, creating a sort of sonic war. It can sound like a beating at some frequencies or a kind of distortion, (an interaction of certain overtones known as wave interference which results in reinforcement

and cancellation of certain frequencies.) There are conflicting overtones and it is therefore unstable to our ears. We hear the distortion and we seek resolution of the conflict into the stable resonance of consonant overtones.

The natural force of dissonance resolving to consonance is the engine that drives western harmony. This physical resolution of acoustical conflict has developed, in the hands of composers and musicians, into the musical cadence—a simple chord progression that gives a sense of resolution or returning to a home chord. The epitome of this is the V-I Cadence, also called the Dominant-Tonic Cadence. A close second is the IV-I Cadence, also called the Plagal or Amen or Gospel Cadence.

This feeling of resolving by 5ths (V-I Cadence) is so strong that we can string them together as a series of resolutions, forming a Circle of 5ths. An example would be a ii-V-I Cadence or a vi-ii-V-I Cadence.

Reading a Chord Chart

The most important thing to know is that when we refer to chords, we use numbers in 2 different ways:

1. **Chord numbers of the key**, such as "the V (five) chord in the key of C." We often use Roman numerals for this, following the classical tradition. More commonly we write the chord letter instead and refer to the number only when speaking about the form or chord

function in the song, such as: "it goes to the IV chord here." (Except for the Nashville Number system, which uses the chord numbers as standard Aramaic numbers.)

2. **Note numbers of the chord**, such as the root, third, fifth, (1, 3, 5) of a C major chord. These numbers refer to the note of the scale and are typically used to signify an upper chord member, such as: a D7 chord, or a G7 flat 13 chord. The are the qualifiers of the chord.

It gets a little confusing when someone says to play a V7 chord, but you get used to it. If there are 2 numbers in a row like that, the first number is the chord of the key, the 2nd number refers to the note of the chord, and specifically which upper note(s) it contains and which may be altered chromatically.

Chapter 1:
Feelin' the Groove
Dominants

[Lesson 37 of Part 2: *The Rhythm String Player* on teachable.com]

The first guitar lesson a kid goes to, they may not know a single chord yet, but they knows how to strum. They can strum the open strings to the rhythm of a favorite tune, sing along and pretend they're playing the tune.

The first thing I would recommend you do as a new rhythm string player is to just play along with some tunes. Find a note that works and play along. You will naturally fall into the rhythmic groove of the tune.

For many classical players it is a real hurdle to get past the idea of just playing without music—the dreaded Improvisation! It may also be another hurdle just to get used to moving in time to the music while playing. Unfortunately, this natural tendency is trained out of many classical string players.

But moving to the beat is the simplest and best way to improve your rhythm.

Rhythmic Music Comes from Rhythmic Movement

Please don't underestimate the importance of involving your whole body in this process of becoming a rhythm player. It is essential to allow yourself to move with the rhythm of the music.

When you see a rock or a jazz band play, they will typically be moving, to some degree or another, in rhythmic unison. Watch their heads. Watch their feet. It helps them play together.

To many classical players, the main kind of moving that is allowed is what I refer to as moving on the **emotional grid**. What I mean by that is moving with the phrase, the way a singer does. It's essentially vocal in nature—expressing a melodic phrase in whatever way is best for that phrase in that moment. Working with the dramatic text, so to speak.

But when I talk about movement being the simplest and best way to improve your rhythm, I'm talking about moving to the beat. Movement on the **rhythmic grid**, as opposed to the emotional grid. Grooving to the beat.

When you see a rock or a jazz band play, they will typically be moving, to some degree or another, in rhythmic unison. Watch their heads. Watch their feet. About 90% of the time, they're all moving together to whatever groove they're playing. That seems totally natural. It helps them play together.

On a more metaphysical note, the music becomes a part of something that is actually larger than just the music itself. When a group of people move in unison together, whether 2 people or a band or a crowd, they are sharing a very particular kind of physical experience. It could be dancing together or marching together, but there is a physical dynamic at work which is very real. The pulse of the music becomes an essential vehicle for this unified communal experience, so don't underestimate that power. Music is only part of a bigger picture.

I think a lot of classical musicians feel that keeping a tempo steady may be boring and mechanical; that you should "do something" with the music. Some may even feel that groove-based music is inherently inferior because it lacks the subtlety of the "emotional grid" and is robotic.

But if you are going to be a rhythm player, you need to bury those classical beliefs because they will only cause you to pull your punches and not break through some barriers you need to break through. If you are going to be a rhythm player, you need to surrender to the power of the groove and prove your subjugation to the force by getting off your chair and moving to the groove before you even pick up your bow.

So, get up and dance!

Feeling Alright

So, here's where we're going to start.

We are going to take a simple 2 chord vamp and just play along.

Dial up Joe Cocker singing "Feeling Alright" on YouTube or whatever streaming service you like, and dance and play along. Or you can use the Play-Along track that comes with the Chord Jams book.

For now, find the note C. That's the only note you're going to play for a few minutes.

(For future grooves that you may want to play with: sing along with the track and find a note or two that works. Then find the note(s) you're singing on your instrument.)

Using your ghosting skills that we learned in The Strum Bowing Method, keep your arm moving in a strumming motion and bring out whatever groove accents you like. You should be grooving along with the music to whatever rhythm you like.

Once that's comfortable, let's try making a little challenge for ourselves, using a few specific rhythms. We'll use the 3 practice grooves that we used for many of the examples in The Strum Bowing Method. These may not really go that well with the track, but we're doing this for educational purposes, so hang with me.

If you look at Chord Jam 1 in the Chord Jams book, Feelin' the Groove, you'll see those 3 practice groove rhythms at the top of the page.

So, play along with the track on the note C, using these rhythms.

Once you're comfortable with these rhythms, I heartily recommend going off into whatever rhythms you like. Make stuff up. That's the whole point.

At the bottom of the page you'll see the chord symbols and the guide notes.

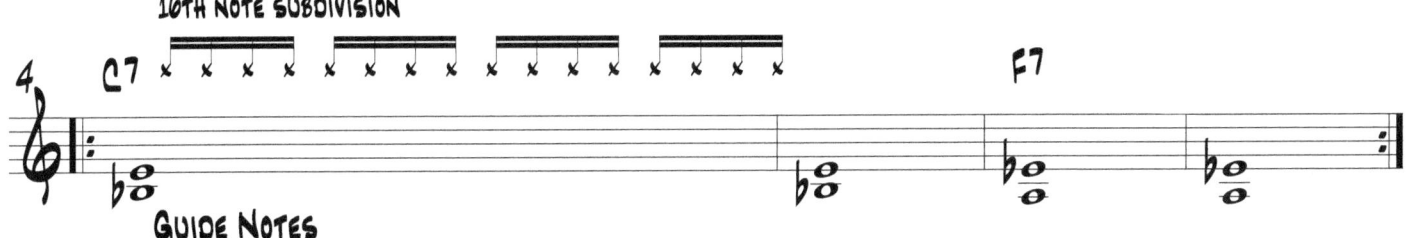

This shows you a few note possibilities for each chord. You could choose one of the notes or play them as double stops. I've written them as whole notes, just to delineate the pitches, but the intention is that you will not play them as whole notes, you will use that pitch and play various different rhythms, according to the subdivision shown above the staff, in this case, 16th notes. You can use the patterns of the practice grooves or anything else that you come up with as you jam with the track.

First there is the 2-bar version, which goes with the tune "Feelin' Alright". I also made a 4-bar version which you can use with the Chord Jams Play-Along track that comes with the Chord Jams book. This is so you have a little more time to jam on each chord.

If you are already familiar with the 3-D Strum, you can play a chop pattern and get as fancy as you like. Or keep it simple and focus on ghosting and muting.

Keep "dancing" while you're playing and remember that you don't have to move much at all to be "dancing."

How to Dance

Whatever it is you're playing, you should be dancing along. If this is not easy and natural for you to do, that's fine. This is often the case with grown-ups. We can fix that.

First, make sure you are alone or somewhere where you don't care who sees you.

Put your instrument down and listen to the tune and dance in place to it. Now, keep in mind, when I say "dance", you don't have to be moving much at all. Bobbing your head, tapping your heel or little things like that totally count as dancing. The idea is for the physicalized rhythm to help you groove, not to distract you, so it has to be movement that is organic to the pulse of the track.

If that works, skip to the next paragraph. If that's not natural, then don't try to move or anything, maybe even sit down, but pay close attention to what you feel like doing when the chorus of the tune comes in and it grooves a little bit harder. How do you move when that happens? Try and go with that small motion and let it guide you. Pay attention to your core and how it reacts. Let that be amplified into your hips and legs and head. Start small and gradually let yourself show the beat physically.

Now take that motion or feeling and hold your instrument like you're going to play. But just dance with it to the track. Hold it like a guitar and strum it. Next, take that motion or feeling and keep it going as you're actually playing a repeated note on your instrument. Keep "dancing" while you're playing and remember that you don't have to move much at all to be "dancing."

It's important to dance first, and then try to play while you're still dancing and keep that feeling. The wrong way is to play first and then try to dance to what you're playing. This is an important difference.

Chords

What's happening chord-wise is what is sometimes called a 2-chord vamp: going back and forth between 2 chords. In this case, they are both dominant chords, that is, a major triad with the flat 7 on top.

A dominant chord always wants to resolve down a 5th. And they also move back and forth very easily, as in this tune, where the dominant resolves down a 5th (or up a fourth to the IV chord) and then seems to resolve right back to the 1 again.

Don't worry if the details of the chord stuff don't make sense. It's much more important that you just hear that there are two different chords going back and forth and to hear that you may need to change some notes in order to play from one chord to the other.

I would also like to point out the guide notes I have chosen for each of the chords are the 3rds and 7ths of those chords. If that doesn't make sense, again, don't sweat it. Just know that the 3rds and 7thds are the chord tones that define the quality of the chord—whether it's major, minor or dominant—so they are a good choice for a rhythm player to use. (We are assuming, for now, that someone else is playing roots of the chords in the bass.)

Enjoy. Remember, if it starts to feel like work, just stop and come back to it later. You don't work a violin.

Groove Prep
Chord Jam 1: Feelin' the Groove

Start by playing one note at a time, then see if you can play double stops. Try to get off the page and just play by ear. Feel free to change any of those Practice Groove rhythms—they're just a starting point.

Chapter 2:
My Sweet Groove
The ii-V Progression

[Lesson 38 of Part 2: *The Rhythm String Player* on teachable.com]

As I mentioned at the end of the last chapter, the most important notes of any chord are the 3rds and the 7ths, because they define the modality of the chord—whether it's major or minor or a dominant chord.

You can think of 3rds and 7ths as toggle switches with 2 positions:

Major Chord: major 3rd, major 7th

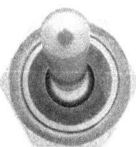 

Dominant Chord: major 3rd, minor 7th

Minor Chord: minor 3rd, minor 7th

Minor/Major Chord: minor 3rd, major 7th
(melodic minor scale)

Play along with the original, "My Sweet Lord" by George Harrison, or with the Play-Along track with the Chord Jams book.

The only difference between this and the previous jam is that this time only 1 of the 2 guide notes move between the 2 chords, where both notes had to move between the 2 dominant chords. Now there is a common note.

Here and for all of the upcoming chapter and etudes, you should use the same pattern of starting by dancing first and then adding your instrument after you have the groove well established in your body.

Also, keep in mind that I have those guide notes written as a good place to start, but feel free to make up anything you like. While you can certainly use the tracks to work on any part of your technique that you like, such as soloing, I am going to challenge you to try to focus what you're doing on strumming simple 1- or 2-note patterns with your bow.

Think like a guitar player. Play double stops if you can, but single notes are fine, too. Just strum along. Keep it simple, don't get fancy. Focus on the pocket—the groove—and try to blend into the fabric of the rhythm section.

Groove Prep
Chord Jam 2: My Sweet Groove

Play along with the track and be free with the groove. There are lots of possibilities. Let your bow wander...

Think like a guitar player. Just strum along. Keep it simple, don't get fancy. Focus on the pocket—the groove—and try to blend into the fabric of the rhythm section.

Chapter 3:
Dominant Strum
Dominants with Toppings

[Lesson 39 of Part 2: *The Rhythm String Player* on teachable.com]

This is the same thing as Chapter 1, in which we went back and forth between 2 dominant chords. We're doing the same thing here but in the more string friendly key of D. The reason we are revisiting it here is so that we can build on it and add some other cool jazz notes—the 9th, 11th and 13th.

Don't get hung up with the math. The 9th is the same thing as the 2 of the chord, the 11th is the 4 and the 13th is the 6.

You can start by using the 3 practice grooves from Chapter 1, but feel free, as always, to explore! Try to work those 9th's and 6th's (13th's) into those chords.

Groove Prep
Chord Jam 3: Dominant Strum

Once you get comfortable with double stops, see if you can add the 3rd note. You can break the 3-note chords into 2 double stops.

Chapter 4:
Honeysuckle Groove
ii-V's with Toppings

[Lesson 39 of Part 2: *The Rhythm String Player* on teachable.com]

In this jam, we're revisiting the II-V progression from Chapter 2, but in a different key and, as with the dominants, with the addition of the "toppings" of the 6's and 9's.

Also, in this one, we double time the chord changes, so that adds a bit of a challenge as well.

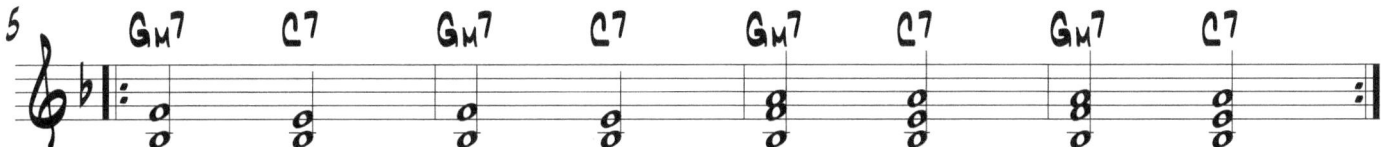

The goal here is to continue to get comfortable with the idea of reading simple chord charts and making up our own grooves within the parameters of the given guide notes.

Don't forget to keep your body rhythmically engaged by tapping your feet, bobbing your head, stepping back and forth, or anything you are comfortable with.

We haven't talked about it yet in this book, but in keeping with my constant reminders to use your voice in The Strum Bowing Method, I'm going to tell you that the more you can sing out loud along with what you play, the faster you will get all this. I know it seems like you should be able to just sing in your head, but unfortunately it doesn't work the same way. It has something to

The more you can sing out loud along with what you play, the faster you will get all this.

do with the cognitive processes in your brain, but, whatever it is, trust me—sing out loud.

And when I say sing, I just mean to vocalize the groove you're playing, like a beatbox or a rhythm guitar riff, or whatever it is that you're playing. Sing along, you'll save yourself some time.

Groove Prep
Chord Jam 4: Honeysuckle Groove

Free yourself to move while you play. Think of yourself as a drummer. Try to keep time with as many parts of your body as you can—nod your head, step from side to side, etc. Physicalize the groove.

Chapter 5:
Groovin' on the Circle
Circle of 5ths

[Lesson 40 of Part 2: *The Rhythm String Player* on teachable.com]

In this chapter, we're going back to the dominant harmony from chapter 3 which included those 6's (13th's) and 9's, but instead of a 2-chord vamp that goes back and forth, this time we're building further on that, using a 4-chord progression.

Western harmony is driven by the idea of dissonance resolving to consonance.

The Circle is Unbroken

The 4 chords in this progression are a string of dominant chords, each of which resolves down a fifth.

As I pointed out in the Introduction to this book, western harmony is driven by the idea of dissonance resolving to consonance.

Chapter 5

In its archetypal form, that is expressed in music as the dominant or V (five) chord resolving down a fifth to the tonic or I (one) chord. We call it a cadence, or an ending.

The all-important 3rd's and 7th's form a very unstable tritone in a dominant chord. It's an unstable interval because the overtones have a strong conflict of frequencies. This drives the need to resolve down a fifth to the tonic. This is also referred to as an authentic cadence in classical music. Dissonance seeks consonance, just as water seeks the lowest place.

Pretty early on, composers figured out that you can daisy-chain these V-I resolutions one chord after the next and create a circle of resolutions that once started, seem to propel themselves onward.

It was used quite a bit by Vivaldi and other baroque composers in the early 1700's and has found its way into music ever since. That's why you'll see this progression in tunes like Autumn Leaves, All the Things you Are and so many others, as well as forming the bridge of "Rhythm Changes."

By the way, because I'm all about myth busting—it was always a mystery to me, when I first started playing jazz, trying to figure out what people meant by "Rhythm Changes". I kept hearing people talking about it and talking about working on it and playing it and I'm thinking, "but the rhythm isn't changing—it's 4/4 the whole time". It wasn't in the Real Book and I couldn't find it on any recordings. Finally, after several years, (this was long before you could google anything,) someone explained to me that it was the chord changes to "I Got Rhythm."

So, I'm happy to be the person to solve that mystery for anyone else. You're welcome.

Sparse vs. Continuous

Now that we're getting comfortable with this routine of reading chord charts with the help of some guide tones, let's start thinking about some other musical considerations.

This same chord progression, because it is so common, is used in jazz as well as rock and funk. The Play-along track to this one is a pretty standard swing jazz groove. If you're playing along with it, try leaving lots of space and being really sparse, the way the piano is on the track. Think ahead about which guide notes you will use and try to be unpredictable about when you're going to play them. This is what is commonly referred to as "comping."

Then try doing the opposite—playing more or less continuously through the chord changes using strum bowing and ghosting/muting to keep a steady groove.

As you're doing this, you will probably start hearing the inner melodies that are formed by following a single voice of the guide notes. These inner melodies are an important part of how you hear and play the harmony and it's a great thing to focus on, and very natural if you're used to playing the inner lines in an orchestral setting. Our classical ear for counterpoint will be very helpful to us in hearing jazz harmony.

Groove Prep
Chord Jam 5: Groovin' on the Circle

Try playing with a swing feel. Then try it with a straight Latin feel. Focus on the descending inner melodies, either as single notes, which can start to feel a bit more melodic, or as double stops. Play with the idea of Percussive Bowing and the area where horizontal and vertical strokes mix.

Chapter 6:
Groovin' Further 'Round the Circle
Circle of 5ths

Lesson 40 of Part 2: *The Rhythm String Player* on teachable.com

This is the same thing as in the previous chapter, but this time in a more challenging key. If you're going to play jazz, you're going to see a lot of flat keys, since saxophones and trumpets prefer the flat keys. So, taking these concepts out of safe "fiddle keys" like D and G will help you feel comfortable when you jump into a jazz jam session in Bb or Eb.

This is in the same key that Sweet Georgia Brown is typically played.

Again, focus on the descending melodic lines. It's always nice when you can combine rhythm playing with a sense of melodic motion as well.

Chapter 6   24

Playing through this a few times will also be getting you more and more accustomed to using those 9th's and 13th's and to hearing those harmonies and melodic lines in your head.

You can also use this as an opportunity to start looking at chord symbols and linking them to muscle memory. Here are few little exercises to keep your brain sharp.

Look at a chord symbol and immediately find the

1. 7th on the fingerboard (instead of the root, which is the intuitive thing to do.)
2. 3rd on the fingerboard
3. 9th on the fingerboard
4. 6th on the fingerboard

Just a few ways you can challenge yourself with these etudes. Also, sing the roots.

Groove Prep
Chord Jam 6: Groovin' Further 'Round the Circle

Again, focus on the descending melodic lines. It's always nice when you can combine rhythm playing with a sense of melodic motion as well. Playing this will also be getting you more and more accustomed to using 9ths and 13ths and to hearing those harmonies in your head.

Chapter 7:
Strummin' Your Way Home
The ii-V-I Progression

[Lesson 41 of Part 2: *The Rhythm String Player* on teachable.com]

In this chapter we're focusing on the ii-V-I progression in 3 different keys. Each one of these could have have been its own etude, but it adds a further real-life challenge to have these 3 different keys within the same etude.

The reference to "home" in the title comes from the resolution of the chords in the ii-V-I progression being like returning home—to a home chord. Let's use the key of F as an example, just cause it's a jazz key we need to be comfortable in.

Here is the ii-V-I in F

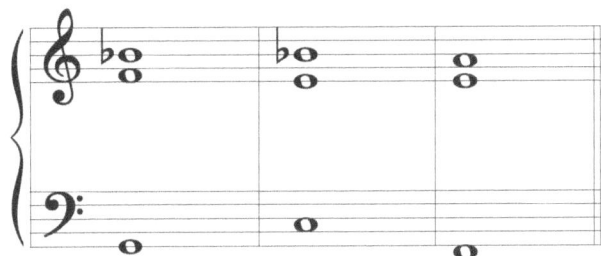

"I'm away from home, I'm almost home, I'm home."

Running Start Towards Home

This is an especially effective way of looking at it when you go back a little further in the circle of fifths and add a few more resolutions before you get to the ii (two) chord. For instance, the chord that resolves down a fifth to the ii chord is the vi (six) chord. So, you often see this chord progression, which is just a bigger chunk of the circle of fifths:

vi-ii-V-I in F

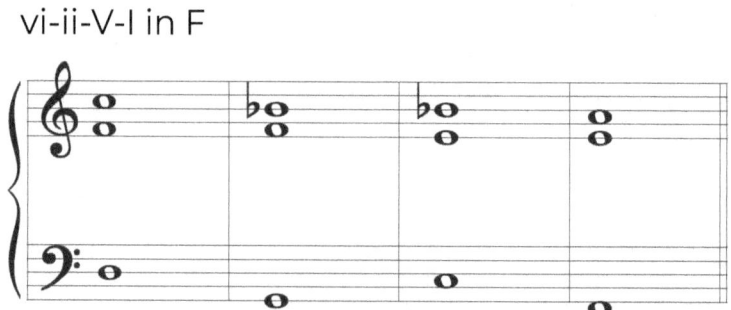

"I'm a ways from home, I'm trying to get home, I'm almost there, I'm home."

And that vi chord can be preceded by it's fifth, the iii (three) chord:

iii-vi-ii-V-I in F

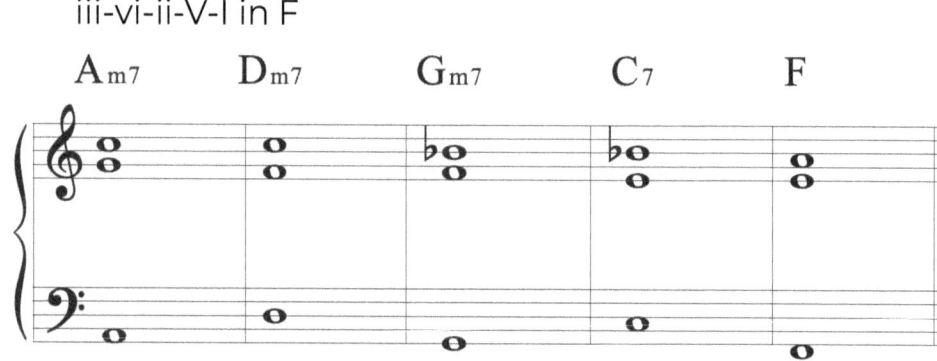

"I'm a long way from home, I'm still kind of far from home, yay I'm getting closer, woohoo I'm almost there, I made it I'm home!"

The little caption beneath each progression is attempting to make the point that by starting at a distance further back on the circle of fifths, you build a greater psychological sense of anticipation, making the resolution that much more musically inevitable and satisfying. It's like getting more of a running start towards home.

The reason it seems more musically inevitable is because it is all **diatonic**. I will explain what that means in a moment, but what is helpful is that our ears already understand this. What this means is that the harmony is consistently giving us cues that point towards a home key. Our ears pick up on the subtle fact that there is a consistent scale or tonality and recognizes the tonal center.

I don't use the vi or the iii chord in etude 7, but it's used commonly enough that it's important to understand how it's just an extension of the circle of 5ths idea of the ii-V-I.

Our ears pick up on the subtle fact that there is a consistent scale or tonality and recognizes the tonal center.

There's No Place Like Home

You may have noticed that I'm adhering to the common practice of using small roman numerals for some chords and large roman numerals for others. The small numerals are used to signify that those are minor chords. This is the difference between the ii-V-I pattern (and its relatives which I listed above) and the circle of dominants that we were working on in the last chapter.

It's a similar but slightly different thing. This is what it would look like if they were all dominant chords:

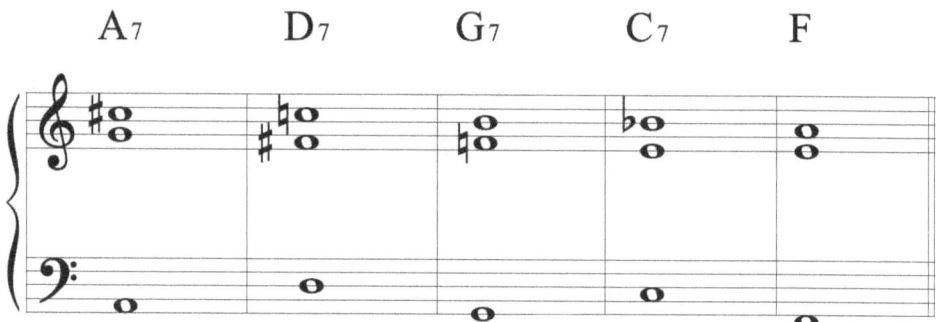

It's similar because it is using the circle of 5ths, but not all of the chords in this chapter are dominants pointing directly to the fifth below. Now, in the case of a diatonic circle of fifths, all the chords are in a single "home" key—thus the "home" metaphor in the title.

The idea is that all the notes for all the chords share a single home key, the tonic or I (one) chord. Or you can say it is all **diatonic**: all of one tonality. And because all the chords share the same scale, some of the chords are minor rather than major or dominant chords—that is, they have minor 3rds instead of major 3rds because those are the notes that come up naturally in the home key.

So, for instance, in the first key of F major, the ii chord is G minor and not G major because the key of F major has a Bb in it, so all the other chords in the key of F will contain those notes of the F major scale, including a Bb.

What that means for the player is that they can play through a whole circle of diatonic fifths without ever having to play more than the one home key scale. So that's good to know. That's a reductive way of looking at it.

From the opposite perspective, you can take any chord, precede it with it's ii-V context, and it becomes its own musical module. This allows for a cubist kind of approach to tonality where you can create mini modulations, juxtaposing unrelated chords using the instant context of the ii-V-I relationship in a small 2-bar musical module.

You can hear this in the bridge of "Seven Steps to Heaven" by Miles Davis, where ii-V-I modules modulate by minor thirds, from C to Eb to Gb:

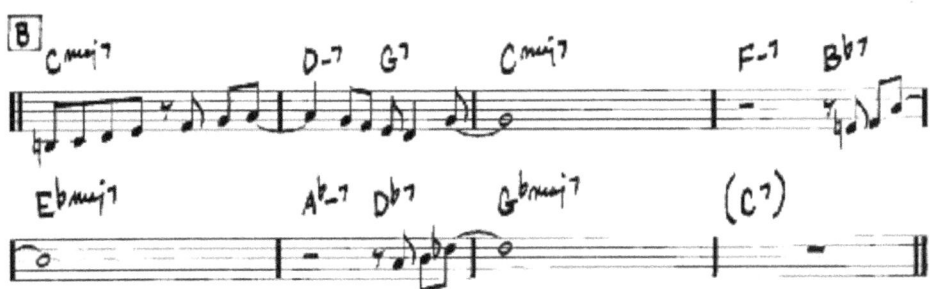

or "Giant Steps" by John Coltrane, where it modulates by major thirds, from B to Eb to G and back to B:

Quite often, just the ii-V part of the module gets used without resolving to the I (one) chord. For this reason, I repeated the ii-V pattern in the Chord Jam etude before resolving it. This is building on what we did in Chapter 4 with Honeysuckle Rose.

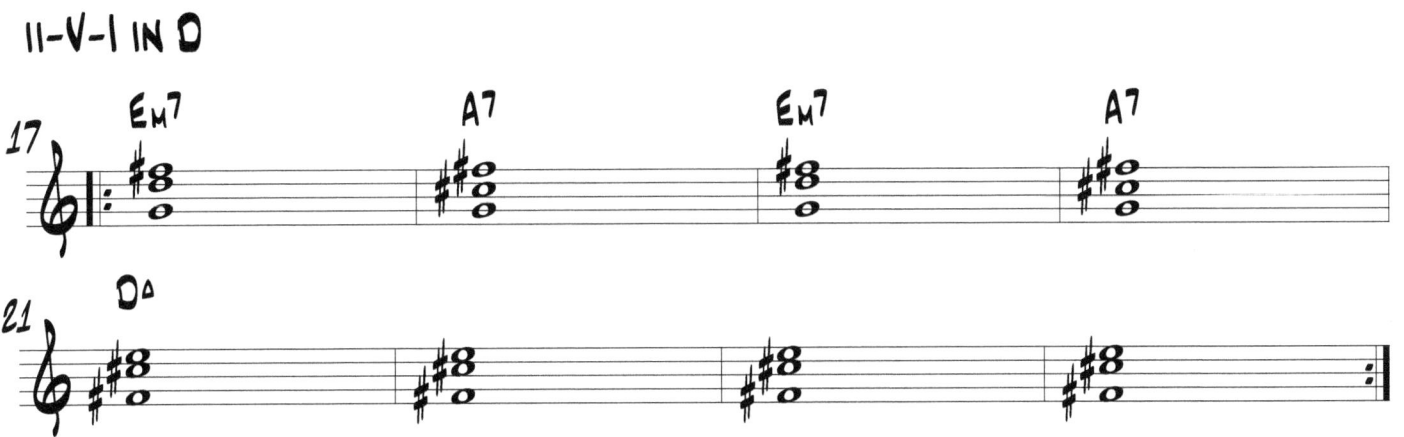

Groove Prep
Chord Jam 7: Strummin' Your Way Home

The goal with this one is to get your hand and ear accustomed to the 3 different keys so that you start to develop some automatic muscle memory. The ii-V-I progression, and just the ii-V part of it, are so ubiquitous in jazz, that it's important to develop this familiarity.

Section 2:
Strum Bowing in Action

Chapter 8:
Sly Strum
Funk

[Lesson 42 of Part 2: *The Rhythm String Player* on teachable.com]

In Section 2: Strum Bowing in Action, we will look at the specific ways of playing rhythm in a few different styles: Funk, Rock, Latin, Folk, Jazz and Hip Hop/Pop.

Different Strokes

Each one of these genres has its own way of thinking about grooves—Latin music is more ensemble oriented, with interlocking rhythms; Jazz is more harmonic, with the emphasis on voice leading (inner melodies); Rock is often based on unison riffs.

I've assembled a couple of examples or generic archetypes in each of these genres which I hope will be the most useful to you. They have differing approaches, to give you the broadest possible palette of techniques to use as building blocks. This is certainly not intended to cover all the stylistic bases, just a few with the idea being to teach you how to apply these ideas to whatever music you love.

The intention is for you to work through all of these different genres and not to skip any. Even if you don't care for a style or ever intend to play it, there is something to be learned from it that you can't get any other way. Your goal should be to have a holistic approach to your instrument and a comfort level across a diverse variety of styles. Even if you don't generally play a particular style, you should understand it. And if you're a teacher, be able to teach it.

As I love to tell everyone, we are better musicians when we know and love lots of different kinds of music, just as we are better people when we know and love lots of different kinds of people.

Guitar and Bass Parts

In all of these examples in different genres, we will look primarily at the rhythm guitar and bass parts. If you like, you can just work on the rhythm guitar part, since that is the main focus of this book. But I challenge you to try to also play the sections which include both bass and guitar.

This makes these Chord Jams substantially more difficult, but working on bass notes as well as upper harmony makes you, first of all, much more aware of the bass and therefore the chords themselves. And it also makes you a much more useful player, able to be self-sufficient as a back-up player the same way a guitar player is able to put together a version of a tune which may include some bass line and some chords in order to more completely represent the tune when backing up a singer. Keyboard players do the same thing. Obviously, this ap-

We are better musicians when we know and love lots of different kinds of music, just as we are better people when we know and love lots of different kinds of people.

plies mostly to 5 and 6-string players, but 4 stringers can cover some bass as well and can always benefit from knowing the bass line.

> Sidebar about bass clef: I use a lot of bass clef throughout the book, so if you are a violinist and not used to it, get used to it. If you don't play piano already to some degree, you should start. I think it's really important for violinists, especially, to play a chordal instrument like the piano or the guitar, because we tend to be very melody-oriented and it's important to have a better sense of what's going on in music, in general. But anyway, learn the bass clef. It's not brain surgery.

I use a lot of bass clef throughout the book, so if you are a violinist and not used to it, get used to it.

Sly Strum

OK, let's quit with the fancy elucidatin' and get with the funkifyin'!

Listen to the classic funk track, "Thank You (Falettinme Be Mice Elf Agin)" by Sly and the Family Stone.

If you're listening, then I will assume you're also dancing, because it's impossible to hear this track and not move in some way.

The function of the rhythm player is not to be fancy and impress. It's to get people to relax and dance.

With a lot of tunes, especially these funk tunes, it's best to start from the bottom up and learn the bass lines. So, the first thing to do is to sing along with the bass line.

Listen to how short the notes are. Try to play it on your instrument. The version for 4-string violin is a bit of a compromise because it's impossible to get to the low D and E, so we substitute with the 5th of the root instead. By all means, go ahead and bounce along with the track and let your body help you emphasize the clipped bounciness of the bassline as you try to recreate it on a string instrument.

Stay close to the frog and keep the bow stroke as small and tight as possible.

Guitar

Listen to the rhythm guitar part in the original recording. Sing along a few times. Then try and recreate it on your instrument.

In the Chord Jams etude 8, I isolate just the rhythm of the rhythm guitar in bars 5-8. This is just so you can explore different registers of your instrument and different voicings for the guitar part. This kind of experimentation is a crucial part of getting the hang of playing these parts. Typically, a part will be relatively easy to play and quite idiomatic to an instrument. If it's not, that's when you have to experiment with different voicings, etc, to find a way to make it feel very natural.

You can copy the exact notes the guitar plays but it may be awkward on a violin or cello. It might be more idiomatic to string instruments to change the voicing—transpose it to a different register, sometimes even substitute different notes if they ring better and are easier and more natural to play.

One of the important differences in the mindset of being a rhythm player as opposed to being a classical player, is the lack of virtuosity. There's plenty of virtuosity in popular genres in the lead players, but the function of the rhythm player is not to be fancy and impress. It's to get people to relax and dance, and usually it helps to be relaxed and dancing yourself, which usually means parts that are natural and easy to play—idiomatic to the instrument.

You want to copy not just the notes, but the ease they're played with.

This is why it's essential to experiment and play with the part when you're copying a song, to make it work for you. You want to copy not just the notes, but the ease they're played with.

That's what bars 5-8 are for.

Combo

Then the challenge is to combine the bass and guitar parts into a single compromise back-up part. This is generally a matter of trial and error and sometimes there are several good ways to do it.

But the essence boils down to this: Sing it first, and whatever you chose to sing is exactly what you should try to play. In other words, you have to prioritize when you are singing, because you can't sing 2 parts at the same time. So, prioritize with your voice, then just try and recreate what you sing.

For this tune, it will likely come out something like this:

Remember that the key is to keep the strumming, the subdivisions, (or Groovons, as I like to call them,) going behind the scene at all times. Since we are at the frog with the bass line, the subdivisions will come out more or less vertically, as a compound chop. If you're not familiar with that term, it's something I talk about a lot in The Strum Bowing Method, and is the vertical equivalent of the horizontal strumming we do in the middle of the bow. It's how we break the chop stroke into fast subdivisions.

Listen!

As you listen to this classic funk track, listen to all the slight variations in those simple parts. Great rhythm players find a way to repeat a basic groove over and over, but always keep it fresh and never make you feel like it's getting stale or tired. It has endless energy and variety, even though it essentially keeps repeating the same thing.

The trick, as you are learning this new style, is to avoid simple imitation of the part—the pattern of notes and rhythms—and to imitate the way the instrument functions in the groove instead—where and how things are emphasized.

Don't just learn a part and stick to it. Learn a function and play with it.

Don't just learn a part and stick to it. Learn a function and play with it.

Groove Prep
Chord Jam 8: Sly Strum

Keep the notes as short as possible by dampening with your left hand. Stay between the middle and the frog for a percussive attack with the bow. Experiment with different notes for the rhythm guitar part in bars 5-8.

Chapter 9:
Soul Groove
Funk

[Lessons 42-Bonus and 43 of Part 2: *The Rhythm String Player* on teachable.com]

Listen to the original recording of the James Brown tune, "Soul Power" (included in the Play-along tracks) and you will understand what it means to groove. Listen to how tight the articulation is. Again, you can't play these notes too short or too dry, in both the guitar and the bass parts. You will have to mute each note by lifting your fingers of your left hand after each note. It's not a technique that is used in classical music, but something rhythm guitar players do all the time.

Keep the bow off the string in that magical area below the middle where it bounces easily but is close enough to the frog to be heavy and close to a chop stroke.

Many funk tunes have a swing feel to the subdivision. Some instruments express that swing more than others. Generally, the drums will swing a little harder than the other instruments. So, it's good to be aware of the swing, but be careful that you don't overdo it.

Groove Prep
Chord Jam 9: Soul Groove

The horn riff at bar 13 is much more legato than any of the guitar or bass parts. It's tricky to switch back and forth between the two at bar 17, but try to stay as low in the bow as you can. At bar 21, be as free with the main guitar riff as you can—try different registers. Explore what you might do as a rhythm player in a jam to support someone who might be taking a solo over it.

Chapter 10:
Get Up and Strum
Funk

Lesson 43 of Part 2: *The Rhythm String Player* on teachable.com

It's also important to play with ease, and that only happens when you play things which are easy for you, so don't ignore the simple fun of jamming on something really easy.

In this chapter we're taking a look at James Brown's "Get Up (I Feel Like Being a Sex Machine)", sometimes called "Get On Up".

First, as always, listen to the track and sing and dance along. Sing the bass line and the guitar part.

We're going to learn it in the original key of Eb so that we can jam along with the recording, but then we will discover how much easier it is to play down a half step in D.

Key Changes

The original key is not terribly string-friendly—E flat. It's good to get used to it, as it's a very common horn key, but it's much more idiomatic for strings down a half-step in D. It will probably demonstrate to you how much better you can groove in a friendly key, and how much better you can groove in general when things aren't too difficult.

It's necessary to practice difficult things in order to expand our technique and ability, but it's also important to play with ease, and that only happens when you play things which are easy for you, so don't ignore the simple fun of jamming on something really easy. In the world of rhythm playing, virtuosity is not such a virtue. Groove is everything. If it feels good, it is good.

Embrace Ease

Another case where the rules are different from the classical world: Embrace ease.

Playing easy things is often overlooked or sneered at in classical studios because it's all about learning the next harder level of virtuosity. There is very little appreciation for playing things which are not necessarily challenging but are just fun to play. But as a rhythm player, you should embrace ease and easy parts within an ensemble. Watch where your attention moves to when it's not occupied with executing difficult technical feats. It often moves to the other musicians you're playing with, and it often finds a way to engage in a dialogue and become playful. Embracing ease is embracing the possibility of being less preoccupied with your own part and more interactive as an ensemble member.

In the world of rhythm playing, virtuosity is not such a virtue.

> Just a little reminder that you will need quite a bit of muscle to articulate the bass notes on these busy funk bass lines. If your arm is getting tired, make sure to take frequent breaks. It may be harder work physically than you anticipated.

Groove Prep
Chord Jam 10: Get Up and Strum

It's time to really focus on getting a dry, dampened articulation. You may be surprised by how much energy it takes to sustain that tight articulation. Playing rhythm is a very physical thing, which is why it's so important to use your whole body—not only to help you keep the tempo steady, but because you need to use the larger muscles in the back, legs and core to keep your arms from developing tension and tendonitis. Let your body help you: keep your arms, wrists and fingers as loose as you can, using the absolute minimum amount of tension, but be free about vigorously engaging the rest of your body. It's a kind of loose-arm groove dance.

Chapter 11:
Riff Rock
Blues Scale in E

[Lesson 44 of Part 2: *The Rhythm String Player* on teachable.com]

Many classic rock tunes are based on riffs that use the blues scale. The blues scale is a minor pentatonic scale with one small addition of the "blue" note, which is the raised 4 or flatted 5.

On upper strings, you can play a one octave minor pentatonic starting with your first finger.

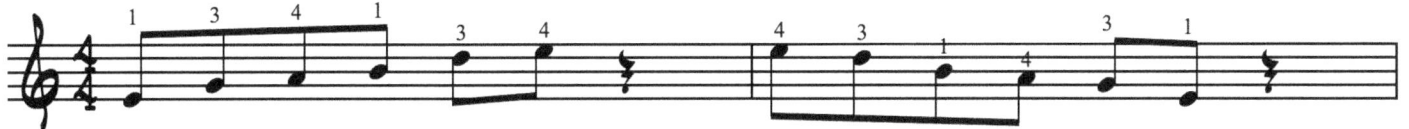

This simple frame or box can be transposed anywhere on the fingerboard.

The Blues Scale adds one note to the minor pentatonic, between the 4th and the 5th of the scale, but could be thought of as more of a gesture than a note—it is a bend or a push/pull of the note.

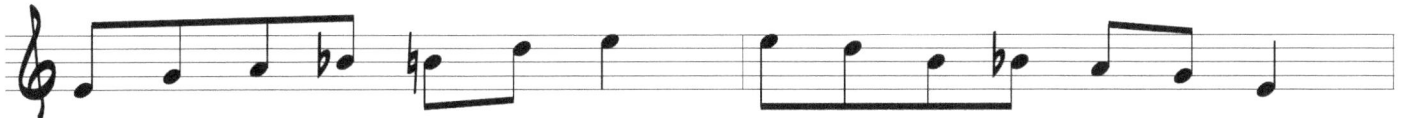

If you add distortion, you'll discover how easy it is to sound like a heavy rock guitar.

Guitar players discovered that, when you play with distortion, you can't play the full chords you might play with a clean sound. Close intervals, especially in a low register, overloads the distortion because of the richness of the overtones, and it turns into noise with little discernable pitch. So, guitar players tend to omit the 3rds and play chords that consist only of the root and fifth—what we call a power chord.

In rock, these power chords could be used for "chugging", which is the equivalent of strumming in that it's fairly continuous, but with distortion. Or power chords could show up as riffs played in 5th's. Examples would be "Smoke on the Water" or "Sunshine of Your Love".

For better intonation, try flattening your finger across the strings rather than approaching it in the more traditional classical way with the fingertip.

Exceptions to the Rules

Starting at bar 17 of the etude, I'm using a bowing for the "chugging" which runs counter to the Strum Bowing concepts that I've been teaching up til now. I'm doing 2 ups in a row so that I can put the accented notes on downbows instead.

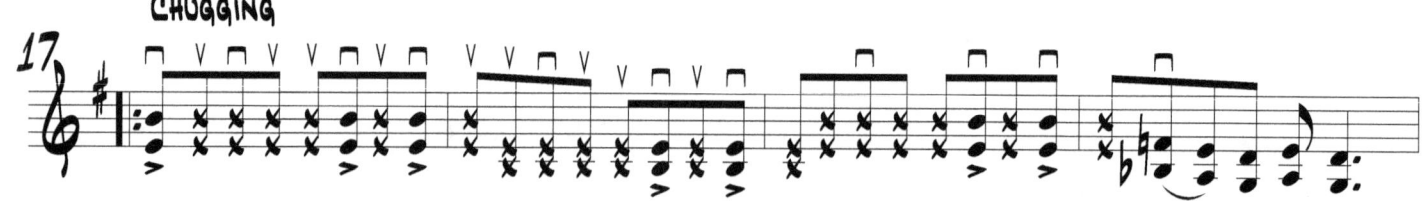

This is a departure from Strum Bowing, which would normally dictate that the bowing would be always alternating down and up bows, so that all syncopations are played with up strokes, all down beats on down bows. And it is possible to play it that way.

But after years of playing rock riffs, I tend to play this chugging type of rhythm with the accents on down bows like this. In this way, it's closer to the "gesture bowing" that I talk about in The Strum Bowing Method. The idea of "gesture bowing" is that you use a down bow for the emphatic accents of the phrase or groove, as you might use a downward gesture of your arm if you were making a point while speaking. That's why it shifts to downbows on the syncopated accents.

But the general concept of keeping all the subdivisions physicalized and played remains from Strum Bowing. At this manageable tempo, it's possible to do two up bows and hit the accents with down bows for more of an aggressive affect.

Groove Prep
Chord Jam 11: Riff Rock

First, get the E minor blues scale in your fingers. I used E because it's the key most use in rock due to the fact that guitars are tuned in E.

The riff at bar 9 bears a striking resemblance to a tune by Cream. Great minds.

At bar 29, make up your own riffs.

Chapter 12:
Jamming with the Geetars
Rock Blues in E

[Lesson 45 of Part 2: *The Rhythm String Player* on teachable.com]

Learning the blues may be the single most useful way to get out of the classical box as a string player. It's so deeply rooted in our cultural ears that we don't really have to learn it, just become more aware of it.

There are whole books dedicated to the blues, so I'm admittedly just brushing the surface here, but at it's simplest, the blues is:
- a short 12 bar form consisting of 3 4-bar phrases
- generally in an AAB pattern, lyrically and melodically
- consists of 3 chords: I, IV and V

It's good to know that there are several different versions of the blues, from a simple early form to a more complex jazz version. I made a little chart called "Da Blues" in which I've narrowed it down to these 3 versions of the blues. I've left out some of the more complex versions it can go beyond this Jazz Blues, but this gives you a good idea of how the blues form has found a strong presence in many different genres.
- Delta Blues—Robert Johnson, Howling Wolf, etc
- Rock Blues— Chuck Berry , Led Zeppelin, etc
- Jazz Blues—Charlie Parker, John Coltrane, etc

Chord Jams Bonus!
Da Blues

Delta Blues

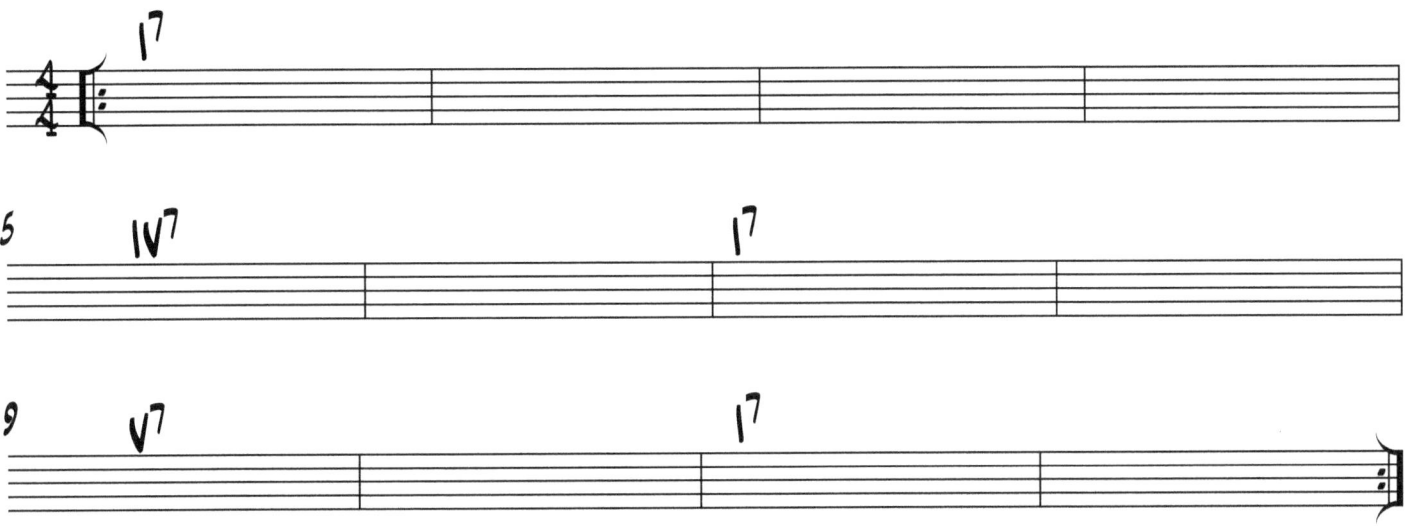

Rock Blues

Jazz Blues

Spend some time exploring playing rhythm on the blues. It may be one of the most useful things you can learn as a rhythm player. Again, just a reminder that you may find it easier to lay your finger flat across 2 strings to help with the intonation on the 5ths.

Groove Prep
Chord Jam 12: Jammin' with the Geetars

You can play this with a straight feel or with a swing feel. If you swing the 8th's, we call it a blues shuffle or sometimes you might hear it referred to as a boogie rhythm, short for boogie-woogie, which was an early form of the blues. If you straighten out the 8th's, it sounds more like early rock and roll, a la Chuck Berry. The harmony of the blues is so well understood by everyone that you barely have to imply the bass notes and the listener will fill in the rest. The Play-Along track starts with a straight feel and then switches to the swung blues shuffle about midway through, at around the 1:30 mark.

Chapter 13:
Cabbage Strum
Bluegrass

[Lesson 46 of Part 2: *The Rhythm String Player* on teachable.com]

We are dealing with the same 3 chords as the blues—I, IV and V— but this time the chord progression is a bit longer. This is a 16-bar tune which will sound very familiar. It's the same chords to "Boil Them Cabbage Down" but in the key of G instead of D.

One of the characteristics of a bluegrass rhythm section is that the bass will alternate between the root and the 5th of whatever chord it is. In other words, if it's a C major chord, the bass will alternate between C and the 5th member of the C major chord, G. If it's a D major chord, the bass will alternate between D and A, the 5th member of the D chord.

Juggling

As before, what we are going to try to do is to juggle the bass line with the guitar line.

The first 16 bars show the chords and all the guide notes. The bottom staves show the bass motion, alternating between the root and the fifth of each chord.

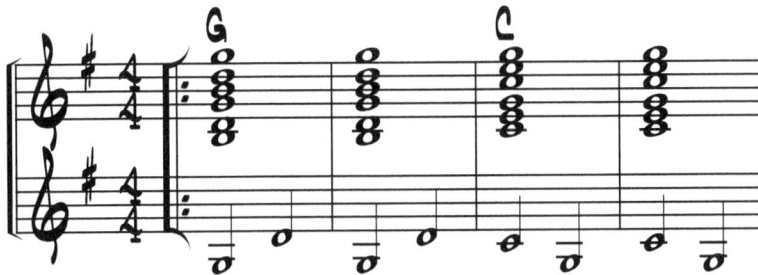

We're going to work on this in 3 stages. First, at bar 17, we will focus on keeping a simple rhythm with the chord tones, mostly on the off beats, and try to add the bass note on the first beat of every other bar if we can.

Stage 2, at bar 33, we are going to simplify the chord tones to a single note but put more emphasis on the alternating bass line.

Then finally, in stage 3, at bar 49, we are going to keep the alternating bass going but add more complicated chord action on top.

Groove Prep
Chord Jam 13: Cabbage Strum

Try to really think chordally. Without a clearly defined melody or riff, your job is to create a functioning harmonic groove that's appropriate to a bluegrass feel. You could sprinkle in some chops on some of the backbeats. As the piece progresses, I add more and more of the 8th note subdivisions.
For the last 16 bars, as always, improvise your own version. Try to add some 8th note subdivisions in there occasionally, (simple scales always work well.) You will have to replace a few bass notes to do this, but then you can jump right back to the bass part to keep the sense of the bass line intact.

Chapter 14:
Drowsy Strum
Celtic

[Lesson 47 of Part 2: The Rhythm String Player on teachable.com]

This etude is based on the well-known Irish tune, Drowsy Maggie. The tune is based on the Dorian mode, (the ii chord,) which is a minor key. As in bluegrass (and as you will soon see, also in most Latin styles,) the bass alternates between the root and the 5 of the chord.

As in the previous chapter, we are going to build from a simple version to a more complex version.
We start with the outline:

Next, at bar 17, play the bass notes where the chord changes and rhythm chord tones in between.

Then we add a little more interest in the rhythm/treble part of the chord.

Finally, use the chord progression and make up your own part.

You may notice that it's easier to play all the quarter notes as downbows. This is so that you can keep a strum of 8th notes going, even if you don't play many of them. This allows you the freedom to drop extra 8th note sub-divisions anywhere you like, because all the quarter note downbeats are down bows and all the 8th note off beats are up bows. Strum bowing at work!

Groove Prep
Chord Jam 14: Drowsy Strum

It's very helpful to sing the bass notes while you play, to really ground your ear and make sure that you are hearing the chords in your head as you are playing them. The bass note is something upper string players are not accustomed to focusing on.

Use short guitar-like bowstrokes that are not too melodic when playing rhythm. Melodic lines tend to be more present and sound more like a solo instrument, so when you are playing rhythm, it's better to be more supportive and less soloistic.

Chapter 15:
Jazz Blues in F
Jazz

[Lesson 48 of Part 2: *The Rhythm String Player* on teachable.com]

First, jazz can be a little intimidating, so do yourself a favor and listen to a bunch of recordings of jazz blues—"Billie's Bounce" or "Au Privave" by Charlie Parker, "Bessie's Blues" by Coltrane, "All Blues" by Miles Davis, etc —and just get familiar with the sound of it. Try to sing the bass lines so you can hear the simplicity of the blues through the various harmonic additions. Like a foreign language, the more you hear it, the less foreign it sounds.

One of the main differences between the Jazz Blues and the Rock Blues is that in the last 4 bar phrase, instead of V-IV-I it's ii-V-I, which is more typical of jazz.

Like many of the other etudes, Chord Jam 15 gets progressively more complex. The guide notes are first just 3rd's and 7th's, then 9th's and 13th's and finally altered dominants of various kinds.

For the 5 and 6-string versions, I've written out a walking bass line because it's very useful to be able to add this into your comping sometimes.

Like a foreign language, the more you hear it, the less foreign it sounds.

Rhythm guitar playing in jazz consists mostly of something we call "comping" which is short for accompanying. Comping is an art in itself. The idea of comping is to support the harmony in an understated way, with a minimum of strategically placed chords. Most jazz comping lines should be quite sparse and rhythmically as angular and unpredictable as possible.

I've written out a possible comp part, but of course this is just one of many possibilities.

COMPING

Start by working on just the comping and then if you want to challenge yourself further, you can try to add bass notes into the mix.

COMPING AND BASS NOTES

There's a lot to absorb here, so if parts of it are a little too advanced right now, come back to it soon and you may be surprised that it has become easier.

Groove Prep
Chord Jam 15: Jazz Blues in F

There are lots of possibilities here for guide notes. I have 3 different versions of guide notes you can pull from. They get successively jazzier as they go, including more of the upper chord tones and chromatic harmony that increases the sense of tension, which in turn increases the power of the resolution.

Try to make interesting melodic lines by connecting guide notes from one chord to the next. You should start with just a single note and then try to add a second note. Then you can try to add more of the guide note tones by breaking or arpeggiating. You can make this as simple or as complex as you like.

Chapter 16:
The Long Way Home
iii-vi-ii-V-I

[Lesson 49 of Part 2: *The Rhythm String Player* on teachable.com]

Earlier in Chord Jam 7, "Strummin' Your Way Home," we played around with the ii-V-I progression. This etude takes that a step further.

We can precede the ii chord by its V chord, (sometimes called a secondary dominant in classical theory, or the V of ii,) which would be the vi chord. And we can precede the vi chord by its V, which would be the iii chord. So, the iii-vi-ii-V-I is a string of resolutions by 5ths (part of the Circle of Fifths) which lands on the 1 chord.

It's a very familiar sound. You've heard it in the classic "Heart and Soul".

All 8th notes are swung, of course.

Inner Melodies and Leading Tones

In Chord Jams 16, The Long Way Home, the first three staves are the same chord progression, the diatonic circle of fifths we learned about in chapter 7. And, as before, each staff gets progressively jazzier, by including upper chord tones and then chromatically altered tones.

Use the Play-Along track that comes with the Chord Jams book. You can use these guide notes to help you form comping lines. Or you can use them to form the basis of a solo.

After the guide notes, you'll see an example of comping written out. And in the remaining slash bars, you should explore your own comping, using the Play-Along track.

Chord Shapes

This is a good time to share with you an important insight into how to play chords, something I think of as the corollary to the bar chord on the guitar—a 3-finger basic chord shape that you can transpose anywhere on the fingerboard.

Groove Prep
Chord Jam 16: The Long Way Home

As in #15, the guide notes get progressively jazzier and I've given you an idea of the comping by itself as if you were playing with a bass player (bar 25) and also how you can juggle the bass line at the same time (bar 41.) Just for fun, try starting with any guide note and letting it either stay the same or move downward in stepwise motion with each chord change, all the way through the progression. You can even keep it going into the next repetition(s) of the progression.

Chapter 17:
Strum Bossa
Latin

[Lesson 50 of Part 2: *The Rhythm String Player* on teachable.com]

The first rule about Latin grooves is that they have straight 8th's as opposed to swung 8th's. The Bossa Nova rhythm developed in the 60's in Brazil and is a kind of cool jazz version of Samba, which is an up-tempo Brazilian dance groove played most notably during Carnival.

As with Bluegrass and Celtic music, the bass will alternate between the root and the 5 on the strong beats, and the guitar rhythm includes a lot of gentle syncopation.

The Magic of the Groove

While most Latin rhythms are very specific, with particular rhythms that are played by certain instruments, Bossa Nova is a bit looser. As you can see from the 5 variants I've listed at the top of the etude, there is a consistent pulse and feel to the groove, but there is actually a fair amount of variety possible.

This is a wonderful demonstration of one of the main precepts of playing rhythm that I talk about quite a bit in The Strum Bowing Method, and that is how important it is to keep the rhythm parts subtly changing all the time, and slightly unpredictable. Otherwise, it stops working its magic on us and we don't respond anymore.

A groove is like a joke—there's an element of surprise. So, the idea is that you never completely know when the accents are coming—the little subdivisions of the groove are always slightly different and force you to not take it for granted and ignore it, but to be constantly affected by it instead.

Tri-tone Substitution

This tune, based on "The Girl from Ipanema," introduces you to the Tritone Substitution. This simply means substituting the all-important dominant chord with its tritone. So instead of the V in a ii-V-I, it becomes a flat ii:

A groove is like a joke—there's an element of surprise.

I've written out the bass line.

We're going to try to do what the guitar does, which is to play both bass and treble parts together. I've written out one possible version of this at bar 51 but spend some time repeating bar 67, where you make up your own with the Play-along track. This type of practice really builds your capability and fluency with chords.

Groove Prep
Chord Jam 17: Strum Bossa

Play through the tune with each of the 5 rhythms shown at the beginning. This style works well in the middle of the bow with a breathy, on-the-string kind of stroke.

At bar 27, I give you an example of how you could realize it with the 2nd rhythm. At bar 35, I'm using the 4th rhythm. Then at 51, we juggle both the bass line and the guitar part. This is typically all done on acoustic guitar with a finger-picked kind of style, the thumb alternating bass notes while the fingers pluck the treble notes. A good example of this style is the guitar playing of Joao Gilberto on the classic recording of the tune.

Chapter 18:
Salsa Groove
Latin

[Lesson 51 of Part 2: *The Rhythm String Player* on teachable.com]

Salsa is a style which originated in Cuba. It's a bit of a catch-all label, like Jazz, but I'm going to use it to distinguish Afro-Cuban music from other Latin styles from Brazil, Venezuela or elsewhere.

All the percussion revolves around a central rhythm key, called the Clave, which is the rhythm in bars 1 and 3. One is just a reverse of the other.

On top of this, many other percussion instruments and rhythms can be layered.

Another important characteristic of Salsa is the Montuno. This is how the rhythm part is expressed in this style. The rhythm part is comping in jazz, or the finger-picking guitar syncopations in Bossa Nova, or chugging power chords in Rock. In this style, it is the Montuno, which is usually played on the piano, often in octaves.

A Montuno is a highly syncopated arpeggiated chord figure and often has a chromatic moving line as part of it.

You should keep your bowing moving in a consistent strum, following the Strum Bowing rules of keeping the subdivision motor running, when playing the montuno.

The chord progression is just a typical 4-chord vamp in a minor key that you might find in many salsa tunes.

Incorporating the bass line with the montuno is difficult but not impossible. Bars 51-70 give you an example of how to pull this off. Strum Bowing is very helpful here, to keep the groove consistent.

A Montuno is a highly syncopated arpeggiated chord figure and often has a chromatic moving line as part of it.

Montuno and Bass Line

You can also try playing the groove closer to the frog, including a chop back beat.

Groove Prep
Chord Jam 18: Salsa Groove

First play through the clave and other rhythms using notes from the guide tones. Then get comfortable with the Montunos at bars 19 and 27.

The bass line is a bit more complex than the simple alternating style we've seen and has a very distinctive syncopation or "push" of its own on the 4th beat.

Putting the Montuno together with the bass line is not easy. I would recommend you slow it way down and practice with a metronome, getting faster one notch at a time. Tried and true.

Chapter 19:
Get Groovy
Pop

[Lesson 52 of Part 2: *The Rhythm String Player* on teachable.com]

The guitar part on this tune is a great example of rhythm guitar playing (by Niles Rogers) and a perfect vehicle to demonstrate Strum Bowing. You keep the steady motor running in your arm and bring out the accents.

The main guitar part is at bar 15:

It makes a good vehicle for practice, so I broke it down and isolated the rhythm of the guitar at bar 9 (a simplified version of it is at bar 10 so you can clearly see the underlying hemiola)

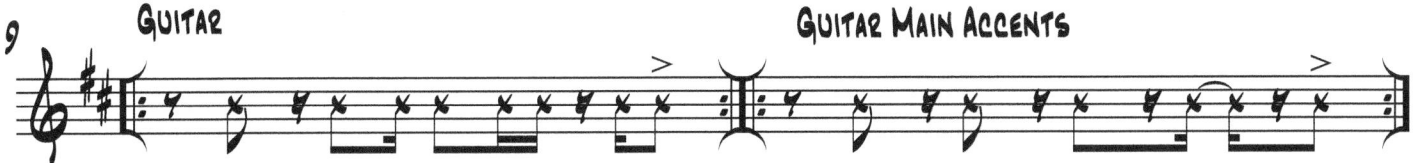

and the Guide Notes at bar 11:

At bar 11, you can use the same format of plugging the guide notes into the groove and explore other voicing (note) possibilities. Play along with the track and see what you come up with.

Notice how the guitar part is repetitious but always effective because it is constantly changing in subtle ways that don't disturb the groove, but keep it fresh.

Keep your bow stroke tight and your notes as muted as possible. This is just like the funk tunes we worked on earlier. Try to keep it as dry as possible.

Groove Prep
Chord Jam 19: Get Groovy

The rhythmic device that powers the tune is the tension and playfulness between the very straight up and down march-like bass part and the very syncopated cross rhythm in the guitar. I think of this as the yin-yang of rhythm—the balance between downbeat energy and upbeat energy.

Once you get both of these feels down separately, try and combine them as I do in bar 19. It's a compromise, for sure, but good practice. Play along with the record.

Chapter 20:
Groovy as Hell
Pop

[Lesson 52 of Part 2: *The Rhythm String Player* on teachable.com]

The challenge for strings is that we can't just copy our part from the record like a guitar player or a bass player can. For one thing, we are playing instruments which aren't included in a rhythm section in the first place because the sound of strings is too old-fashioned and classical. So, we have to overcome our natural classical sound and people's natural predisposition to reject a string instrument taking over a guitar role.

Secondly, the guitar or rhythm parts we are trying to replicate may not be terribly idiomatic to our instruments. Making it even harder is the fact that our closest cousin, the guitar, is not used as much in contemporary pop music as it used to be back in the heyday of rock and roll.

So, while we are learning these tunes and these riffs, don't expect that what you play has to sound just like the record. It won't. It's something new. It's not a drum, it's a violin being played like a drum. It's not a guitar, it's a cello being played like a guitar.

Our goal is to capture the rhythmic groove of a tune and interpret it on our instruments in a way that is both authentic to the style and idiomatic to string instruments. I refer to this as **post-classical** string playing.

> *Our goal is to capture the rhythmic groove of a tune and interpret it on our instruments in a way that is both authentic to the style and idiomatic to string instruments. I refer to this as **post-classical** string playing.*

As before, we want to keep the articulation and bow strokes as tight as possible and to dampen the strings as much as possible to keep them from ringing. This is especially true because we are in the key of Ab major and our open strings will not sound good.

Groove Prep
Chord Jam 20: Groovy as Hell

Keep the articulation crisp by dampening with your left hand. Lift your fingers almost off the strings immediately after playing notes to mute them. Try to capture the subtle swing feel. It's a tricky shift of gears to go from the heavy rhythmic drive of the groove to the melodic vocal part in bars 12 and 14. Don't allow the groove to be disturbed in any way when you do this. Play along with the record or with a metronome. Better to leave out a note or two than to alter the beat in any way to accommodate the difficulty. This is always true for playing grooves.

The steadiness of the groove is sacrosanct. You don't get to slow down when it's hard or speed up when it's easy. There is no rubato of any kind when playing a groove. Its power comes from the inevitability of the pulse. A groove represents eternity.

Chapter 21:
Vibrato and Stuff

[Lesson 52 of Part 2: *The Rhythm String Player* on teachable.com]

One last word about an important part of your playing as a string player—vibrato.

My best advice about vibrato in pop music is...don't use any. The use of vibrato is very different from the classical vibrato—something much more intentional and sparse.

The use of vibrato in a pop music setting is a somewhat contentious and subjective issue among string players, so I will preface this by simply saying this is just my opinion. Feel free to disagree. But it's my book, so I'm going to tell you what I think.

My best advice about vibrato in pop music is... don't use any.

Vibrato—Your Musical Accent

Your vibrato is like your accent when you speak: it reveals where you're from. As a musician, I believe your vibrato should be controllable and used intentionally in a way appropriate to the style of music you're playing, and not an automatic part of everything you play.

Just as an actor will adjust their own native accent to suit the character they are playing, if a musician plays in more than one genre, they should use a vibrato that's appropriate to that musical role. An actor may be from Brooklyn and have a heavy NY accent, but if they are playing a character who comes from Barcelona, they

I believe your vibrato should be controllable and used intentionally in a way appropriate to the style of music you're playing, and not an automatic part of everything you play.

will not be terribly believable without some attempt to lose their native accent and adopt a different, Spanish accent.

The same is true in music. If you were raised with Brahms and Tschaikovsky, you will probably have developed a lovely classical vibrato which is your native accent. But that vibrato is completely anachronistic and (I think) somewhat ridiculous when playing a pop tune. It's like an opera singer using their beautiful classical vibrato to sing a Cardi B song.

Now this is where it gets subjective, because there is a valid argument to be made that it is an artistic choice to use your native classical accent as a way of defining yourself as an artist who is from outside the genre deliberately bringing a classical perspective to the pop song. Fine.

But if it's not a deliberate artistic choice, then more than likely the muscle memory of your native vibrato simply hasn't ever needed to speak with a different accent and has not done the long-term work that's needed to break down the deep muscle memory of vibrato and develop other alternative vibratos, or be able to play with no vibrato at all.

Would you play a Mozart concerto in the same style as the Brahms concerto? If not, you may want to develop different vibratos for music outside the classical realm as well. I recommend learning how to play without any vibrato at all and then relearn a variety of different vibratos by closely imitating the vocalists and instrumentalists in whatever style you're playing—saxophones in jazz, guitars in rock, and the singers in any genre.

The Car Alarm Exercise

In order to develop a new vibrato, we need to establish new muscle memory while not slipping back into your old muscle memory. The best way to do that is to start broad with a very different type of motion and then refine it gradually so that by the time it becomes a more subtle motion, it is distinctly different from your classical vibrato.

In order to develop a new vibrato, we need to establish new muscle memory. What we're going to do is to slide our finger up and down the string like a light glissando. Keep it light or you will get a string burn on your finger because we are going to be doing a very wide vibrato at first.

The main difference between this type of vibrato, which is the basis for jazz and rock styles, and a classical vibrato is that in a classical vibrato, your finger is planted more firmly, pressing the string all the way down to the fingerboard, and your finger rolls back and forth, creating a very narrow and fast vibrato. Here, we are lightly sliding up and down the string, like a mini-glissando. It's slower and wider. Also, it is used more occasionally and intentionally and less automatically. Much of the time, there is no vibrato used at all.

Would you play a Mozart concerto in the same style as the Brahms concerto? If not, you may want to develop different vibratos for music outside the classical realm as well.

Chapter 21

So, take any finger, place it on a note and do a glissando up an interval of a 4th. When you do this, plant your thumb behind the neck and pivot on it as you reach your hand up the 4th for the glissando. Don't shift. It will almost look like you are waving your hand at yourself.

Remember to keep the slide very light, like a harmonic. And normally I would want the thumb to follow along with the hand when shifting, but in this case, as I mentioned, the thumb stays put and you slide your hand back and forth. In actual use, the gliss will not be so exaggerated. We start out that way only so we can differentiate it from our the muscle memory of our classical vibrato.

It should sound super annoying, like a car alarm siren. Little by little, you will decrease the distance of the glissando from a 4th to a major 3rd, a minor 3rd, major 2nd, minor 2nd and finally a micro-tone. But the way you are moving your hand, sliding it up and down the string as opposed to rolling it on the string, is the main difference that you want to retain, even as the motion gets smaller.

Many string players are very adverse to playing with no vibrato. It's a tough sell because they are afraid of a few different things. First, without vibrato, you have to play in tune. Vibrato is like a filter in photoshop or Instagram. It can soften all the edges and make everything sound kind of in-tune-ish. And also, we are afraid that we will sound like a beginner who hasn't learned how to play with vibrato yet—we will sound amateurish. Also, to most classical ears, the violin simply doesn't sound sweet unless it has vibrato, even if it's in tune. It's too plain without it.

But that's because you're used to hearing the violin in a classical context. Try to imagine if you had never heard a string instrument before. And someone picked one up and played it the way Miles Davis plays the tune "Blue in Green"—tenderly and intimately but without a shred of vibrato.

Different Rules for Different Schools

It's difficult to abandon our conception of what a violin should sound like—the concept of beauty that has been a given since we started playing our instruments. But if we listen carefully to the instruments in jazz, rock, hip hop and any other contemporary genre, we will hear a different use of vibrato, tone, timing and many other things.

There are different rules for different styles, and when we are playing our string instruments in contemporary genres, we have to try to make them sound more like the instruments in that genre—the guitar, keys and percussion—rather than the old classical instruments we are accustomed to.

We are not losing our old accents and our classical techniques, we are simply learning a 2nd language of pop music.

We are not losing our old accents and our classical techniques, we are simply learning a 2nd language of pop music—post classical string playing.

What is ironic and challenging is that the popular music that we are learning as a second language is what non-string playing musicians have learned as their first language.

What is ironic and challenging is that the popular music that we are learning as a second language is what non-string playing musicians have learned as their first language.

The Future of Strings

But this is not an insurmountable obstacle. As string players, we can easily copy what we hear being played in all these non-classical styles. We just need to be armed with the knowledge that

- we will have to make some fundamental changes in our playing
- we have been given permission to use a different set of rules

This means we need to think differently about how we want our instrument to sound and what we consider beautiful. A distorted electric guitar playing a power ballad can be beautiful in a very different way from the Sibelius violin concerto.

So, even though you will need to work out all the details of technique on your instrument, the most important shift you ever make as a string player may not be between positions on the fingerboard, but in your way of thinking about what your instrument can do.

Here's to opening the minds of string players to the future of strings as rhythm instruments as well as a melodic ones.

Closing Words

In your quest to be a rhythm player, one important skill is to be able to keep a steady beat. Engaging your body is key to this, as I've written about earlier. But you can also think of it as a sense of balance that comes from being perfectly comfortable or at ease with what you are playing—you aren't slowing down, you aren't speeding up, you are just right where you are.

This can happen at many different tempos, and the key is to find that balance and ease that allows you to stay exactly where you are. It's like you are planted into the earth and can't be moved.

Keep in mind that rhythm playing is not about virtuosity, it's about groove. Sometimes very simple things can feel great. To a string player, accustomed to a life of struggle just to make pleasing sounds, it may seem too simple. It's not. Sometimes it doesn't take much. At other times, it needs to sound simple but may actually be really awkward at first to pull off on a string instrument. It may take a while til there's any sense of ease and comfort.

But give yourself some time to repeat these grooves over and over. Take all your newly-gained ease and comfort and this new awareness of groove steadiness and revisit some of the earlier Chord Jams. Customize them to feel more comfortable. This is one of the wonderful parts of playing in a non-classical context. You get to play whatever feels good to you, to make it your own in a way you may never have gotten to do before with classical

the most important shift you ever make as a string player may not be between positions on the fingerboard, but in your way of thinking about what your instrument can do.

The only rule is that the groove reigns supreme.

music, where your job is primarily to play what's on a page. Explore this new freedom! The only rule is that the groove reigns supreme.

If it feels good, it is good. And if it doesn't, keep groovin' til it does.

Glossary

3-D Strum: A combination of horizontal and vertical strumming.

Back Beat: The second and fourth beats in a 4/4 meter.

Bowing Key: The bow directions determined by Strum Bowing; the bowing that results when you add placekeeper notes to a phrase and impose a constant down/up bowing grid, then remove the placekeepers but retain the bowing.

Chop: Also referred to as the Simple Chop; a non-pitched vertical bow stroke consisting of a down stroke and an audible up stroke.

Compound Chop: A double-time version of the Simple Chop in which the first note is stressed and the other 3 are not.

Dampen: To mute the string by touching it lightly with a finger of the left hand without producing a harmonic.

Feel: The personality that you bring to a groove; those subtle intangibles of timing and dynamics that create a rhythmic character.

Gesture Bowing: Emphasizing with your bow arm the way you might if you were speaking emphatically.

Ghost Notes: The unstressed notes in a groove; dropped notes; nearly inaudible pitched or non-pitched sounds; the opposite of accents.

GPS for Strings: A method for learning how to play new grooves with Strum Bowing. The four steps are:
1. Hum It—Get It in Your Voice: Vocalize the Groove
2. Strum It—Get It in Your Body: Find the Groovon
3. Say It—Get It in Your Brain: Discover the Bow Direction
4. Play It!—Get It on Your Instrument

Grid: A consistent framework that helps keep rhythms evenly aligned; a rhythm ruler; a.k.a. The Groovon Grid.

Groove: A consistent subdivision of the pulse defined by a pattern of accented and ghosted notes.

Groovon: The smallest particle of a rhythmic groove; the smallest usable subdivision of the beat; a Groovon is to a beat what protons and neutrons are to atoms.

Montuno: a highly syncopated arpeggiated chord figure, usually played on piano and often including a chromatic moving line. It is the Salsa equivalent to a strum.

Physicalize: To actualize your inner drummer, i.e. to express the subdivision physically as a strum or other motion; to allow your body to respond to a groove with movement; to dance to the groove.

Placekeeper Notes: Ghosted subdivisions that fill long notes or rests and keep you properly aligned on the grid.

Pocket: Another word for groove or feel. Drummers and bass players often refer to being in the pocket or having a great pocket.

Power Stroke: The first, heaviest stroke of the Compound Chop.

Pulse: The beat. For instance, in 4/4 time, there are four pulses per measure.

Rest Stroke: The third, unstressed stroke of the Compound Chop.

Strum Bowing: Using your bow like you're strumming a guitar.

Subdivision: 1) The act of dividing a pulse evenly into smaller increments. For instance, a quarter note can be divided into four sixteenth notes.
2) A fraction of a pulse.

Swing: The unequal subdivision of a pulse, in which the first note is typically twice as long as the second, creating a triplet. The amount of swing can vary from a subtle unevenness to a "hard" swing.

Syncopation: Accenting a normally unaccented up beat. It usually has the feeling of anticipating the following beat.

photo: Eric England

For play-along tracks for every etude in this book, and for all things Strum Bowing related, please visit **Strumbowing.com**

If you'd like to work on these etudes with me, please visit my online courses: **strum-bowing-groove-academy.teachable.com**

For information about workshops/clinics/residencies, teacher training, online lessons, speaking engagements or performances, you can reach me at **info@tracysilverman.com**

Please visit me at **tracysilverman.com** where you can sign up for my newsletter, The Scuttlebutt.

Follow me at:
Spotify: fanlink.to/spotify-TS
Instagram: @tracysilverman
Facebook: TracySilvermanMusic
Twitter: @tracysilverman
YouTube: youtube.com/tracysilverman

Grooooooooooove on!